EXPLORING
CAREERS IN
TV AND FILM

Costume Design in TV and Film

Nancy Capaccio

Cavendish
Square

New York

Published in 2019 by Cavendish Square Publishing, LLC
243 5th Avenue, Suite 136, New York, NY 10016

Library of Congress Cataloging-in-Publication Data

Names: Capaccio, Nancy.
Title: Costume design in TV and film / Nancy Capaccio.
Description: New York : Cavendish Square, 2019. | Series: Exploring careers in TV and film |
Includes glossary and index.
Identifiers: ISBN 9781502640383 (pbk.) | ISBN 9781502640390 (library bound) |
ISBN 9781502640406 (ebook)
Subjects: LCSH: Costume design—Juvenile literature. | Costume—Juvenile literature.
Classification: LCC PN2067.C37 2019 | DDC 792.02'6--dc23

Editorial Director: David McNamara
Editor: Kristen Susienka
Copy Editor: Rebecca Rohan
Associate Art Director: Alan Sliwinski
Designer: Christina Shults
Production Coordinator: Karol Szymczuk
Photo Research: J8 Media

Printed in the United States of America

CONTENTS

In the 2017 version of *Beauty and the Beast*, a classic story is told anew, with the Beast in costumes created with computer-generated imagery.

CHAPTER ONE
Design World!

Have you ever heard of a job where you don't want your work noticed? For costume designers working in movies and television, an important measure of success is how well the costumes help tell the story without becoming a distraction for the audience. However, this isn't always the case. For superhero shows and films, the costumes have a starring role and typically receive a good deal of buzz and tweets. If you close your eyes, you may be able to picture Wonder Woman, Black Panther, or Thor.

Another genre in which costumes get plenty of attention is "period dramas," also known as "costume dramas." For the TV series *Downton Abbey*, for example, scrupulous attention was paid to the cut of the coat, the sweep of the gown, and the style of the hat each character wore.

What's It All About?

The art of "costuming" is much more than sewing clothes. Costume design involves a wide range of skills, of which sewing is just one small part. Costume design is also different from fashion design. A fashion designer routinely creates entirely new garments. She or he has a brand or a style that their fans recognize and value. A costume designer for film and television, on the other hand, only sometimes creates entirely new garments. The costumes that appear in futuristic or sci-fi movies like *Black Panther* or *Star Wars* have to be created from scratch. But for more conventional productions, the costume designer is more likely to rent garments or buy clothing, which may have to be altered or transformed to suit the characters.

Acclaimed designer Deborah Nadoolman Landis, who has worked on classic films like *The Blues Brothers* and *Animal House*, clarifies an essential difference between fashion and costume design: "Costume design has far more to do with storytelling than to do with clothes. Fashion is the polar opposite of costume design because fashion is all about the clothes ... My job is about *creating the person* who's wearing the clothes."

Through costumes, the designer helps tell stories about characters, family, social conditions, and way of life, and "dresses" the changes in the principal characters as the story unfolds. The designer shows

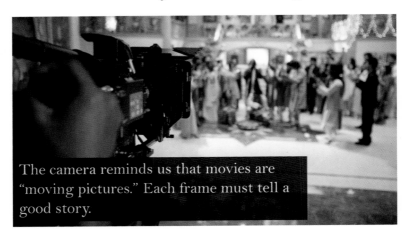

The camera reminds us that movies are "moving pictures." Each frame must tell a good story.

us the characters' strengths, weaknesses, feelings, and idiosyncrasies. By creating harmonies and contrasts among the characters, the designer clarifies relationships and intensifies the drama. All of this is done to express the director's point of view.

The costuming process is not limited to designing and collecting clothing but entails a range of related activities—from creating the wardrobe used in the production to managing the budget, keeping up with the shooting schedule, and making sure the costumes are delivered to the set on time. There are many ways to participate in the world of costume design.

The primary focus for costume designers is the characters involved in the production. But that's only part of the story. A costume designer, whether working in film or television, must consider a number of other elements in order to be effective:

- The performer, whether an actor, an extra, or a stunt double

- The world of the script, such as eighteenth-century France or the starship *Enterprise*

- The set, such as a sandy, windswept planet

- The camera, with its tendency to flare white colors or flatten the image

- The shooting process, typically out of order (for movies)

- The viewing format, such as a smartphone or the big screen at the theater

Goals

Even if you are designing for a school script-based video, you can strive to meet the same goals as a professional costume designer. Here are some of the goals to keep foremost in mind as you explore costume design:

1. Make each character come alive. Judianna Makovsky, known for her work on many movies in the Marvel cinematic universe, including *Avengers: Infinity War* and *Guardians of the Galaxy Vol. 2*, along with *The Hunger Games*, says, "Most people are not aware that it's about designing a total person, not just clothing. I'm designing a character from head to foot."

2. Make the clothes look believable. You want the audience to believe that these characters are wearing their own clothes.

3. Draw the viewer's eye to the main characters, just as in theater. Kimberly Adams, who designed the TV series *Stranger Things*, gives an example: "Ted Wheeler, Nancy's father, is a less significant character and therefore he dresses very nondescript, allowing him to blend into the background."

4. Design differences between the characters according to their status and roles. In the *Ocean's* trilogy, Matt Damon's character (Linus Caldwell) is the youngest and most

inexperienced of the group. So, at the start of *Ocean's Eleven*, we see him in loose, relaxed clothing complete with a baseball cap. It's only later that we see him wearing a suit and tie, which signals his growth.

5. Make the costumes either unnoticeable or the star. Surprisingly, one of the best compliments a designer can receive is, "I didn't notice the costumes."

6. Design clear differences between groups. Renowned designer Michael Kaplan explains: "When I first saw [the original] *Star Wars*, I was … confused about which army I was watching. [So when designing *The Force Awakens*] I created two definite color palettes and fabric-type divisions … The New Order colors are cold: black, shades of grey, teal blue, and … white. The fabrics are polished wools, nylon, and synthetics … The Rebel color palette is earth tones: olive drab, rust, tan, ochre and shades of brown. The fabrics are natural: cotton, boiled wool, linen."

7. Create and work within a color palette that meets the vision of the director and the production designer, and the period and tone of the script. While working on *The Hunger Games*, Makovsky "used more color than I've ever used in my entire life, it's a very controlled and tight palette. Otherwise, the screen becomes a mish-mash, like a bad painting."

8. Create costumes that are lightweight and comfortable, yet strong enough for the role. While soldiers in medieval times may have been grateful to wear chain mail, actors today are not. They want it lightweight, so their chain mail is merely knitted cotton that has been sprayed silver. Who knew?

Impact

An immediate impact of the designer's work is how well the clothing supports the actor in becoming the character. Kimberly Adams enjoyed the process of discovering the *Stranger Things* character of Barb with actor Shannon Purser, saying, "We tried on lots of clothing, but when she put on that first ruffled plaid blouse, we both looked at each other and knew we had found her! When you see the actor become the character in the mirror, it's really rewarding."

Whether in a movie or a TV series, costumes change as the story moves forward; they help signal the advancement in time. Additionally, costumes may change to reflect the emotional development of the character. Actor Shailene Woodley, who played main character Tris in *Divergent*, values the contribution that her wardrobe makes in telling the story: "You know, they're not just pieces that the characters wear. They're almost characters within themselves. They help to tell the story visually."

Yellow Light

As the head of the design department at the Fashion Institute of Design and Merchandising in Los Angeles, Mary Stephens points out that the most challenging aspect of fashion design is that it is "a highly technical industry, requiring great attention to detail and patience." The same is true for costume design.

A desire and ability to work well with others is another core requirement. Oscar-nominated designer Mary Zophres, who designed the costumes for the musical movie *La La Land*, exclaimed: "I love the collaboration of it all. It's also very important to love actors and to love the process of turning them into their characters, and I do!"

Mary Zophres holds an award at the Costume Designers Guild Awards in February 2017.

Another must-have is flexibility and the ability to work at a fast pace. So if you're wondering if this field is for you, ask yourself: Do I thrive on an adrenaline rush?

Costume design is a highly competitive field. Large production companies, for both film and television, typically hire union workers; the unions are hard to get into. As a novice, you may have to pay your dues by working as an intern or working for free for a small, independent production.

Bottom line: If you want to be a costume designer, you need to be a fan of clothes, stories, and people. You also must be able to function in high-stress situations and be willing to make some sacrifices in the beginning of your design career.

Skill Set

Here's what folks in the field say are valuable assets for would-be designers, along with tips on how to improve your skill set while you're in school:

A Good Eye

That means a good eye for detail as well as for color, style, design, and fashion history. Having a good eye is generally regarded as the one indispensable quality that a costume designer must have. You need to visualize the costume from different points of view: on the actor, in the context of each scene with other actors, on the set, and within the entire film. To sharpen your eye for detail, you can watch shows for inconsistencies in styling and post them on the internet.

A Talent for Drawing

Sketching can be learned, so why not start now? It's not a career-ender if you can't draw, since illustrators are available for hire.

Ability to Visualize

When reading the script, it's valuable if the costume designer can visualize the set and the interaction between the characters, including the extras ("atmosphere" or "background"). You can hone this skill by creating "mood boards" for scenes in the books and stories you are reading for school. A mood board is a collage of images that represents a feeling, concept, or look.

Versatility

While some designers choose to specialize in one genre, your value can grow as you demonstrate an ability to be effective across genres. After the World War II drama *Pearl Harbor*, Kaplan did the action comedy *Mr. & Mrs. Smith*, followed by a *Star Trek* movie, and then a musical. Talk about being versatile!

As you study literature, challenge yourself to find illustrations of the clothing worn in each period. You'll find sources in the For More Information section in the back of this book.

Imagination

When the director of *Looper* told costume designer Sharen Davis that he wanted his futuristic film to look nothing like *Star Trek*, she came up with the novel solution of rejecting all jewelry and instead using hair and makeup to signal wealth and status.

Attention to Detail

Makovsky speaks fondly of her work on *Harry Potter and the Sorcerer's Stone*: "The ghost costumes including Nearly Headless Nick are amongst my favorites. Every piece of trim on Nick's Elizabethan costume was stenciled on sheer ribbon, every button embroidered. I wanted something that was not the usual floating white ghosts. It had to be substantial and ethereal at the same time, also period accurate."

Stamina

A willingness to "work hard and fast" is a frequently heard comment from people in costume design. That's necessary when you're a set costumer who has to stylize twenty-five extras or a tailor who has to make a dozen duplicate jackets for an upcoming shoot.

Understand Storytelling

Janty Yates, designer for *Alien: Covenant*, *The Martian*, and another thirty movies, advises: "With film design you have to climb into the story and allow it to absorb into your bones. To be authentic, the designer has to run the timeline and the character arc [the character's

Costume designer Michael Kaplan used a muted color palette for the rebel characters, including Rey and Finn (pictured here), in *Star Wars: The Force Awakens*.

development over the course of events]. You have to live and experience each character's history."

Why Do It?

Given the fast pace and hard work required in costuming for film and television, why do it? Designer Betty Pecha Madden, with extensive experience in both film and television, relays that "It's the only career that I haven't gotten bored with." Like others in the field, she admits to being an adrenaline junkie. She adds that every script is "a new adventure" and loves that the people she works with—from producers to directors to the talent—are always presenting her with a brand-new set of challenges.

Costume designer Patricia Field collaborates with actress Meryl Streep for *The Devil Wears Prada* in 2006.

CHAPTER TWO

Collaboration

Teamwork has an important role to play in costuming. Even more vital is collaboration. In costuming for film and television, there are several types of relationships at work. The costume designer looks up to the producer and director for approval; across to the cinematographer and director of production; and leads the wardrobe supervisor, who is in charge of the people hired to make the costumes and work on set.

Decision-Making Players

People in the following positions have the authority to approve or disapprove of the costumes for a production: director, producers, production designer, cinematographer, and lead actors.

Director

The director's vision is *the* critical part of the equation for movies. While the script tells the story, it is the director who envisions how the story is going to be brought to life. Some directors can be extremely specific. Ryan Coogler, who cowrote and directed

Black Panther, drafted the color palette to be used by his very experienced costume designer, Ruth E. Carter. He specified using the black, red, and green colors of the Pan-African flag, assigning black to T'Challa—the Wakanda royal who is also the Black Panther—red to the warrior Okoye and her band of female fighters, and green to the spy Nakia.

Producers

In television, in contrast to movies, it is often the producers, rather than the director, who will have the first say in the design process. A key role of a producer is to think about the cost of the production versus the business goals. For television, the goals are high ratings and advertising revenues. For movies, the goals are a film's potential box office and profit margins.

Given their role, it is easy to understand why producers are increasingly likely to encourage (or demand) the use of "product placement." In exchange for loaning (or possibly giving) designer-label or famous-brand clothing, companies will receive a screen credit. While the prop master may be encouraged to get a Porsche in a product placement deal, a producer may encourage a costume designer to get garments from Ralph Lauren or some other well-known clothing designer.

Production Designer

The production designer is responsible for the look of everything you see, from location, sets, and props to the decorations on the set and special effects.

The costume (or wardrobe) department, along with the makeup and hair departments, reports to the production designer.

A production designer is a critical collaborator in the costume design process, as he or she has a wide range of expertise, covering color theory, history of design, interior design, lighting, cameras, and lenses. In selecting fabrics that will work for the production, the costumer may need to collaborate with the production designer. Designer Sharen Davis explains:

> In movies with African-Americans [such as Antwone Fisher with Denzel Washington], white fabrics against dark skin is a big issue. Working with the production designer, I test at least ten variations to establish the standard white for clothes, sheets, aprons, curtains, everything, because it really will not work on screen if all the whites are different. We try to use the same gray or tan tech [dye shade] throughout the film design.

Cinematographer

The cinematographer, often called "the DP" for director of photography, wields tremendous power during the shooting. Everything waits for his or her crews—camera, electric, grip—to prepare for the next shot. As we'll see in chapter 3, holding up shooting while the costume department gets mustard out of the leading man's tie can be a nightmare.

It's the cinematographer who knows how to light a scene in a way that presents the right mood, provides depth (to avoid visually flattening the scene), and shows the fabrics and surfaces as they are meant to be seen. Here's how Kaplan describes collaborating with the cinematographer on *Star Trek*:

> From time to time, there might be an entire scene that is being shot in close-up, and you can't see much of the costume. I try to have conversations with the cinematographer beforehand to say, "This is a very special costume that needs to be seen for these reasons. If we can, we should show it from the feet up."

Lead Actors

Ideally, the lead actors approach costume design as a collaborative effort. One such actor is Johnny Depp. Depp establishes a close rapport with the designers who help him bring to life characters as distinct as Edward Scissorhands, where Colleen Atwood was the designer, and Captain Jack Sparrow, whose costume Penny Rose designed. Depp has said, "It's always great to have that layer of the character's clothing—the skin. It helps you find your posture [and discover] how does the character stand?"

In working with lead actors, the smart designer wants to give the actor choices. For the first film in the *Pirates of the Caribbean* series, designer Penny Rose selected what she thought were eight great pirate hats.

As Captain Jack Sparrow in the *Pirates of the Caribbean* movies, Johnny Depp's costumes were more rock star than real pirate.

Depp immediately picked up the leather one, saying "That's mine." Rose explains: "He knew instantly which was the correct hat for his character."

In a truly collaborative relationship, the actor may sometimes inspire the designer. When Depp first met Rose, he said he thought Captain Jack Sparrow was "a rock-n-roller." She based the character's famous costume on rocker Keith Richards of the Rolling Stones.

Actor Robert De Niro so appreciates the role of costumes that he retains his own costumes to donate them to the Harry Ransom Center at the University of Texas in Austin to aid in the study of costume design. Currently, there are about eight thousand costumes, props, and makeup items from fifty-six motion pictures and two theater productions in the Robert De Niro collection.

Celebrity actors may voice objections to the costuming, creating a need for negotiation or accommodation. When Harrison Ford was reviewing sketches for *Blade Runner*, he was clear that he did not want to wear a hat. Why? Ford had just finished

Director Lasse Hallström and costume designer Jenny Beavan on the set of *Casanova* in 2005

filming *Raiders of the Lost Ark*, in which he had worn a hat throughout the entire movie.

Feedback from the actors can be very practical, such as informing the designer that something doesn't fit comfortably. The crew in *Alien* was originally wearing regular helmets until the actors became claustrophobic, so air holes were added.

Animation and Visual Effects Teams

In movies that feature animation, it might come as a surprise that the animators have a strong voice in approving costume designs. Joanna Johnston, an Oscar-nominated and highly regarded designer, wanted the animated character Jessica in *Who Framed Roger Rabbit* to wear a fully sequined gown throughout the film, but the animators objected because such a gown would be too time-consuming to animate and would run their costs over budget. They compromised: Jessica's gown would only appear to be sequined when she was singing on stage—other times it would be a plain, red, satin gown.

"Chroma key" is the effect commonly used when shooting, for instance, an announcer that appears to be standing in front of a satellite photo or a weather map. The announcer is actually standing in front of a "green screen," which is a single color, typically ultra matte green or "chroma key blue." (Can you guess why green or blue? If you answered, "Because those colors are not found in skin tones," you're right!) If chroma key blue is being used, then anything with that color, or tones close to it, will "disappear." In that case, if you're designing costumes for a weather forecast, be sure your announcer isn't wearing a blue turtleneck—unless you want him to look like his head is floating!

Other Collaborators

There are other professionals with whom costume designers work, but with them the goal is to earn their cooperation rather than their approval.

Writers

While in movies the scriptwriter is typically not involved in the costuming process, for television, costume designers often have a working relationship with the writers. Says Ann Foley, costume designer for Marvel's *Agents of S.H.I.E.L.D.*:

On my show, I work really closely with the writers to make these characters identifiable based on their costumes. Sometimes, when I get the script, the description of the costumes is right there on the page and then it's my job to help bring that to life. For Agents of S.H.I.E.L.D., *there are some existing designs from the original Marvel comics; for new characters, I rely on the writers to give me insight into who the character is, so I can design a costume that makes sense.*

Hair and Makeup

The head(s) of the hair and makeup departments have been conceptualizing their own designs at the same time as the costume designer. In fact, for some productions, iconic hairdos are critical to establishing the time period. For example, *Stranger Things* is set in the 1980s, when mullets and too much hairspray were signs of the times.

There needs to be collaboration to come up with a complete look that represents the character. Makovsky appreciates this teamwork:

The projects that I enjoy most are those where I have a collaborative relationship with the hair and makeup team ... Before hair and makeup come on board a project, I do lots of research and create inspiration boards ... Most people are not aware that ... I'm designing a character from head to foot, and that includes hair and makeup. When hair and makeup [stylists] arrive, they give me even more ideas for the actors. That's how it should work.

Often, the character's appearance will need to evolve as the story develops. For example, in episode 7 of season 2 of *Stranger Things*, the character of Eleven gets a punk makeover courtesy of her "sister," Kali. Kim Wilcox, the new designer for season 2, needed to work with the hair and makeup stylists to create a look that was punk from head to toe. Wearing a blazer with rolled-up sleeves and a bandana on her wrist got Eleven only halfway to a punk look. She needed heavy black eyeliner and slicked-back hair to complete it.

Art Department

The designer also collaborates with the art director, who also reports to the production designer. The art department is responsible for the creation of the sets and the transformation of locations on a production.

In designing for TV, especially episodic television, the art department is an important point of contact. If the designer joins after the project has started, which is not uncommon for series that are renewed, the art director will provide the color palette being used. Checking with the set decorator clues you in to such things as upholstery fabrics. You don't want to dress your leading lady in a beige suit only to have her disappear as she sits on a beige sofa!

DANCING WITH THE STARS

Howard Sussman loves his job as costume supervisor for the hit TV show *Dancing with the Stars*. He doesn't design the dresses that the celebrities wear, nor does he glue all those Swarovski crystals—as many as fifteen thousand!—on the gowns. Instead, he functions as the team leader responsible for getting the designers, seamstresses, and assistants to do their best work, so that the costumes are all delivered to the talent trailers exactly two hours before the start of the live taping of the show. Then the costumes must

Dancers perform during the season finale of *Dancing with the Stars* in 2015.

be ready not only to flatter the dancers but stretch and twirl.

Sussman's workweek shows how important each person is to making this popular show dazzle its audience. On Tuesday night, after the results show, the designer consults with the remaining couples to conceptualize their "look" for the next show. On Wednesday, it's time for the designer and the so-called shoppers to, well, shop for fabrics. They discuss the designs and turn over the fabrics to the wardrobe head and tailoring shop.

Sewers get to work on Thursday, and fitters meet with the talent for their first fitting. Specialists experienced with beading and fringe get started after that. All day Sunday is spent with the celebrities doing fittings. Set costumers will deliver the finished garment to the trailers on Monday afternoon at four.

The men and women dancing on stage look sensational, thanks to a whole team of people who are devoted to making them look good. And the team gets to enjoy working with celebrities and seeing their work broadcast to adoring fans.

Mood boards contain fashion swatches so designers can create wardrobes that provide both variety and continuity.

CHAPTER THREE

Telling the Story

Now we're ready to dive into how the costume designer contributes to telling the story by transforming actors into characters and scripts into moving pictures. We'll follow the steps in the process as it is done for movies, since that is the most extensive.

While movies are shot over months, and large productions begin preplanning years before the release date, shows for television use very tight schedules, which require design shortcuts. Other differences in television productions will be pointed out as we go.

There are four phases in the costuming process:

Phase 1: Preproduction: Conceptualizing

Phase 2: Acquiring the Costumes

Phase 3: Principal Photography

Phase 4: The Wrap

Phase 1: Preproduction: Conceptualizing

Preproduction for costuming may run a few weeks to a few months or more because there is a lot to get done. For *Black Panther*, preproduction began one year before shooting.

It all starts with the director hiring the costume designer. The designer, as an independent contractor, then hires the rest of the team. Together, the designer and their team will create and manage the final wardrobe.

A crucial member of the team is the assistant costume designer. This person will function as the designer's eyes and ears in the workroom where costumes are being built, in fittings with the actors, when shopping and pulling costumes from stock, and on the set.

The designer will typically hire a costume illustrator, who will be responsible for creating visual representations of the designer's concepts. The illustrator often partners with the designer on a daily basis, during preproduction and the actual shooting. Unless it is an independent production, all three of these people will be members of the Costume Designers Guild.

The next key member of the team is the costume supervisor, or "super." This is the person who will set up and run the wardrobe department. Some say the designer does "the look," while the super "makes it happen." The costume supervisor and his or her assistants will belong to the Motion Picture

Costumers union for film and television. All major productions hire union members; the wages and the responsibilities of each job are very specific. The union in turn determines how its members may or may not help each other, which can make collaboration challenging, especially for people accustomed to a team environment where everyone pitches in.

The Design Concept

Understanding the director's vision for the production is the first step toward developing the design concept. For a movie set in the past, the designer will have to decide whether the production will aim for "period authenticity" or try something different. For Captain Jack Sparrow in *Pirates of the Caribbean*, the designer chose "something different." Instead of dressing Johnny Depp as a seventeenth-century pirate, she took her inspiration from Hollywood swashbuckler movies of the 1950s. Actual pirates from that time period would hardly recognize Jack Sparrow as one of their own.

Research Process

After consulting with the director and understanding the overall vision, the designer will get to work searching for materials that can serve as the basis of the costuming. At this stage of the process, it may be too early to create any illustrations for actual costumes. The designer's main focus is to come up with a plan that will support the director's vision while giving form and shape to the designer's own vision of the end results—the "look" of the costumes.

Paintings, such as this early eighteenth-century French portrait, inform designers about historical clothing, textiles, and colors.

As designers and their assistant designers do their research, they are collecting images not just of the clothing people wore but also of the overall look and feel of society at the time. From this collection, they create collages called mood boards to share with the director, producers, and production designer to arrive at a common vision. The script tells them what is happening in the story. The mood boards communicate the look and feel of the story as they work to bring it to life.

Research is required not only for productions set in a historical period but also for contemporary work. To create her mood boards for the series *Stranger Things*, designer Kimberly Adams researched a creative array of materials: movies and television shows of the period, plus catalogs, magazines, family photo albums, and 1983 yearbooks from the Midwest. Notice the specificity of her choices: not all yearbooks from the 1980s but rather just those from the Midwest for the year 1983.

Designer Ann Foley clarifies the importance of script analysis and research: "The job [of designing] is more about research than it is about fashion. You have to know how to design clothes, but more importantly, you have to understand who is wearing them and why." While one goal of the research process is to understand the look of a time period, whether contemporary or historical, another important goal is to understand how people within that time period dressed differently, according to their status, job, age, and more.

For their research, designers use valued compilations in book form with such titles as: *Power Dressing: Textiles for Rulers and Priests* and *Showing Status: Representation of Social Positions in the Late Middle Ages*. There's also *The Complete Costume Dictionary* by Elizabeth J. Lewandowski, which includes more than twenty thousand fashion and costume terms, making it the most comprehensive resource available today. The volume covers costuming through the ages and around the globe; it also features more than three hundred illustrations.

Websites provide quick access to a range of images and patterns. Sewing patterns are available at sites like reconstructinghistory.com, which can be useful for your school or independent productions, for cosplay, or simply to learn more about the garments worn during different historical periods around the world.

Creating the Character

How does a costume designer go about creating the character who is wearing the clothes? After reading the script several times, the designer and assistant begin a detailed analysis of the script to refine the design concept and apply it to the characters. This particular script analysis—and there will be more to come—has four objectives:

1. Identify the circumstances in each scene, such as the social status and profession of each character. Watch for any eccentricities.

2. Check the scene-to-scene flow of the script. How does the mood change? What scenes are pivotal? In season 3 of *Agents of S.H.I.E.L.D.*, designer Ann Foley dropped the use of patterns and colors so that the simpler clothing would signal the characters' post-traumatic condition.

3. Track what drives the action. How can the contrast among characters' clothing increase the impact? For example, if the leading man is dressed to appear more vulnerable than his rival, will the fight be more compelling?

4. Look for ways to heighten the emotional impact of the action on an audience. How might the drama be heightened with color choices, such as darkening the color palette as the hero becomes lost?

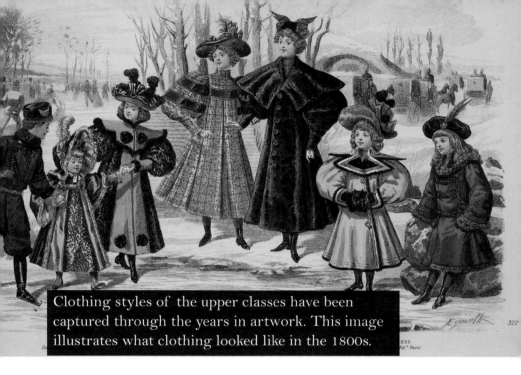

Clothing styles of the upper classes have been captured through the years in artwork. This image illustrates what clothing looked like in the 1800s.

Design

Working from the approved mood boards and sketches, the designer and illustrator now get down to creating the very specific renderings of the costumes. These sketches are important not only in winning the director's approval of specific costumes but also for made-to-order (MO) work. Sketches showing front views, back views, realistic proportions, costume details, and the character's attitude help the people building the clothes do their work accurately. As part of this process, the design assistant will be gathering swatches (pieces of fabric) for the MO work. A variety of fabrics will be collected to determine which will work best for each character, scene, and color palette. These are shared with the production designer and sometimes the cinematographer, as fabric color appears different under different lighting conditions and as captured by different media (film or digital).

Breakdowns

Having completed a close analysis of the script, the designer is ready to undertake another script analysis—called a "costume breakdown"—that will determine how many costumes are required for every scene. It will take into consideration such things as key actions that affect costume condition and count, including stunts, progressive damage and distress, and the need for stunt and photo doubles.

This sketch shows an outfit for Audrey Hepburn's character from the movie *Sabrina*. It was designed by costume designer Edith Head.

For example, action sequences requiring stunt doubles will mean creating multiples, or identical versions, of the same costume for each sequence. For the movie *Collateral*, twenty-six copies of one suit were made for Tom Cruise and his three stuntmen.

The costume department typically uses five different types of costume breakdowns. Each one uses a different set of costuming requirements: by character, by scene, by costume, by script page, and for the entire script. Using the breakdowns, the designer can now create an extremely detailed budget. Here is one more place where the ability to pay attention to details is a critical skill and where the ability to use spreadsheets is especially helpful. If you don't know your way around a spreadsheet, have a friend give you a tour. Better yet, offer to keep track of the budget for a club activity.

Budgeting requires not only attention to detail but also persuasiveness. In defending her proposed budget for costumes for *The Lord of the Rings*, designer Ngila Dickson recalls: "When I said I was going to need a minimum of ten versions of Frodo's costume alone, everybody tried to shoot me down in flames." Actually, she needed even more. For each version, extra copies had to be built for Frodo's body double, stunt double, and horse double. Plus, his scale double needed it reproduced in a small size but as an exact match down to the rips and tears. Frodo was played by both 5-foot 6-inch (168-centimeter) Elijah Wood and by 4-foot 1-inch (124 cm) Kiran Shah. The production cast two sets of actors (one shorter, one taller) to portray the hobbits, dwarves, men, and elves.

Now that both the designs and the budget have been approved, it's time to acquire the costumes.

Phase 2: Acquiring the Costumes

Will the costumes be "built," purchased, or rented? During the designing and budgeting process, decisions will have been made as to whether or not the costumes will be built, i.e., custom-made. For example, if the leading man will be wearing a jacket that gets torn, then renting it is out of the question. And if he is wearing it in several scenes, you'll want at least one multiple. Even more multiples are needed if he will have a stunt double or a "photo double." A photo double is a lookalike actor that may be used for something like a wide shot where he's just driving away from a scene.

Shopping and Pulling

Shopping for costumes for a movie or a television show is similar to everyday shopping. But there are differences. For starters, the people shopping for costumes are using someone else's credit card. They are also buying a variety of items to provide options for both directors and actors to choose from. Remember Depp and the eight pirate hats?

Thrift shops are great places to shop for contemporary or twentieth-century clothing. Items already look worn, so the need for aging is reduced. More importantly, you can achieve that 1980s look, for example, by finding items that were actually made in the 1980s. One drawback is that if there is a need for multiples, you'll have to make them yourself.

"Pulling" is the term used for selecting items from the studio's wardrobe collection, or, more likely, from a "wardrobe house." A wardrobe house is like the costume-rental store that supplies outfits for Halloween and local theaters. The world's biggest is London's Angels Costumes. It rents out its 1.5 million costumes for film, theater, and television productions around the world. To help you find what you need from the 8.5 miles (14 kilometers) of clothing racks, there are 120 assistants on staff.

The Construction Process

Before you started this book, you might have thought about "costuming" as sewing clothes. While you now understand that sewing is just part of the process, it's a critical craft with possibly many professionals involved.

In the first half of the twentieth century, film studios had huge workrooms for creating costumes. That is no longer the case. Instead, if a designer decides on made-to-order costumes, she or he often needs to set up a workroom with everything from scissors to sewing machines to personnel. If the production requires materials that can't be purchased or rented, the designers can turn to costume houses that offer that service. Their skilled tailors can make alterations and construct individual garments, such as suits or dresses, for the principal actors.

Take a look inside Angels Costumes, the largest costume supplier for the entertainment industry.

The size of the workroom staff depends on the scale of the production and the number of costumes that will be needed. A workroom supervisor, hired by the costume designer, will add one or more of the following highly skilled specialists: patternmaker; cutter or fitter; stitcher or seamstress; tailor; draper; dyer; ager or distresser; and textile artist.

For a really big production, the designer may have the time and budget to also make the fabrics. A recent example of this would be *Black Panther.* Big-budget pictures may require subcontracting to get the work done. For *The Lord of the Rings,* a factory was set up in China with two thousand workers to manufacture lightweight chain mail from thermoplastics (a material used in car bumpers).

Distressing and Breaking Down

Costumes should look used, like something the character pulled out of their closet or trunk and put on that morning. If actors only wore newly purchased or freshly made clothing, they would look like a walking clothing catalog. People in the movie industry criticize such looks as "too TV." (Television shows with a limited budget and fast-paced production schedule tend to rely on newly purchased clothes.)

Another reason for making new costumes look "experienced" is to integrate them into real vintage clothing that has been rented or pulled from company stock. You may have created this effect yourself if you ripped up your jeans so they would not look new.

In most movies or TV shows—even those with contemporary settings—characters will only appear

A seamstress adjusts a costume after an actress has been in for a fitting.

authentic if their costumes look "lived in." The boys on *Stranger Things* don't look like they are wearing brand-new sneakers—but they are. The costume department bought new sneakers and then distressed the shoes so they look like they really belong to the boys. The specialists who do this work are called costume "agers" or "distressers."

How do they do it? Aging is accomplished by sandpaper, sponges, spray bottles, steel brushes, awls, dye, bleaching (fading), glue, spray paint, matches, cigarette lighters, motor oil, cooking oil, food coloring, Kensington gore (movie blood), and Fuller's earth (sterile movie dirt).

When working with Brad Pitt on *Se7en*, designer Michael Kaplan found an old leather jacket in a thrift shop, then had it manufactured in multiples because it would be damaged in fight scenes. Since the jackets needed to appear secondhand, distressers aged each one by breaking buttons, cracking the leather, dyeing, and washing them. As a result of this process, the jackets ended up looking thirty years old, even though they were actually made the week before.

Testing

Remember the importance of establishing a good relationship with the cinematographer? That is valuable during preproduction when smart designers have fabrics tested under shooting conditions. Both the lighting and the choice of media (digital or film) affect how fabrics will look to the audience, a fact that designers who have worked in theater quickly learn. The camera captures colors differently and can be confused by certain patterns. Designers train themselves to see what the camera sees, which helps them know beforehand which costumes or fabrics will need to be tested.

Do you think this is vintage or a heavily distressed new jacket? What makes you think so?

If you're shooting a film for school or with your friends, notice how colors change. For example, some smartphones amp up the green to produce more intense pictures of landscapes.

For *The Help*, set in Mississippi in 1964, while domestic workers wore white uniforms to clean houses, testing revealed they looked like nurses. So the designer (Sharen Davis) switched to the color gray, which gave their uniforms the desired look. (Growing up in Louisiana, Davis had seen her own grandmother wearing a gray domestic worker's uniform when she went to work.)

Many dramatic moments occur in dimly lit or nighttime scenes. Oscar-winning designer Colleen Atwood provides a tip she used for Grant Gustin's costume as The Flash that you can use when you shoot in low-light situations:

> *I played around with different colors applied to a darker surface to give it light when moved at certain angles, because if you get it too dark you don't see any detail. So you have to be careful to have some kind of highlight to it or capacity for it to light when it's in a night situation.*

Testing can also involve checking to see how the fabric moves. For the *Divergent* film series, a new fabric was invented for the Dauntless faction. While the fabric appeared flexible, the costumes needed to be tested to make sure it would do the job in action scenes. The testing showed which costumes needed additional gussets—patches of fabric sewn into a seam to allow for extra movement.

Fittings

Actors go through a series of fittings so that the clothes fit as well or as poorly as they are meant to do for each character. Of course, the actor's ego is also involved. Oscar-winner Mark Bridges, who has dressed Jennifer Lawrence, Woody Harrelson, and Juliette Lewis—to name just a few—puts it like this: "You'll get an actor to approve a costume if they look good but it makes them feel like somebody else. It's an elusive combination … They know they're going to be forty-feet [12 meters] tall on the screen, and they're worried about the size of their behind, no matter how famous an actor they are."

Fittings are not for everyone. Actors are ranked according to their importance in the production, and this ranking determines whether they will be fitted. The most important actors are the "stars," whose casting allows the producers to raise the necessary funds to produce the film and get distribution deals. Next are "principals," who get a lot of screen time. Stars and principals have a say-so at their fittings, and experienced designers go out of their way to work well with them. At the third level are "featured players," also known as "day players" because they are only on set for a few days. Those are the three sets of actors who have their costumes fitted.

Individuals who work as "extras" are also called "atmosphere" or "background." Extras may or may not

Downton Abbey was called a costume drama because the costumes were so important to its appeal.

be fitted, depending on the nature of the production. Typically, they bring their own clothes to a shoot and allow the designer to choose the appropriate outfit; they are paid for "renting" the clothing to the production. Alternatively, the designer will use costume stock for background performers. If any productions are shot near where you live, try to get cast as an extra so you can work with these specialists, who are called "set costumers" because they work with the actors and their costumes on set.

Phase 3: Principal Photography

Let's start off with the most important rule for the costume department while on set: "production should

Actors on the *Big Bang Theory* TV show act out a scene, each wearing a costume unique to their established character.

not have to wait for wardrobe." Why? Time is money, and lots of it. Everyone is moving as quickly and efficiently as possible, following the pace of the camera department. Even though money is not involved in amateur productions, you can still appreciate how grumpy everyone gets when they are kept waiting.

It pays to know the number of pages of script that will be shot each day, since it sets the pace for your work in costuming. On average, two to three pages of script are shot per day for feature films, while for TV movies, it's about six pages per day.

Each costume is "established" when it is shot for the first time. The designer must be on set when each costume is established to make sure the performers are comfortable and to oversee any costume alterations the director may want. In some cases, the director may request an entirely different outfit. Either way, it's up to the designer and his or her team to deliver the goods.

Continuity

As soon as each costume is established, it is photographed and documented for future reference. During production, recordkeeping is absolutely essential since directors will typically shoot scenes "out of continuity," rather than in chronological order. For example, suppose the movie has several scenes on a beach. All of the beach scenes will be shot together. Maybe their costumes are the same, but maybe they are different. If they are the same, was the star wearing a beach cover-up or not? Was she wearing her sunglasses, or were they perched on top of her head?

Tracking costume continuity is one of the jobs of the "set costumers," who are always present for each day of shooting. This may be a single person or a whole team, depending on the number of actors and extras. They are also responsible for seeing to it that the actors are comfortable, bringing them coffee or water, for example.

If mistakes in continuity amuse you, check out sites like moviemistakes.com to find goofs even in big productions. In *Harry Potter and the Order of the Phoenix*, keen eyes caught Dudley wearing two different pairs of shorts in the same scene. Oops! Somewhere there are costumers who are blushing or out of work.

Remember when we talked about the need for flexibility? One reason for this is that script changes are common. In fact, it is so common that the process is color-coded, with the first wave of changes on blue paper, next on pink, then yellow, then green. Costumers talk about scripts that have been every possible color before shooting ended.

Phase 4: The Wrap

A wrap occurs at the end of every day of filming when the various departments clean and put away their equipment. Costumes are broken down, which in this case means that they are separated, tagged with the name of the actor, and laundered. Yes, the costume department is responsible for washing and ironing everything daily.

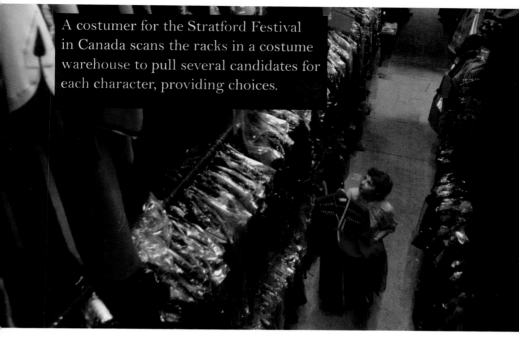

A costumer for the Stratford Festival in Canada scans the racks in a costume warehouse to pull several candidates for each character, providing choices.

The final wrap occurs at the end of principal shooting and involves a final cleaning of the costumes, drawing up an inventory for returning rentals, paying bills, and putting principal costumes into storage at a costume house, studio, or production company.

After the film has had its commercial release, costumes may be sold to the public by eBay or auction, sold to costume rental houses for stock, or placed in costume stock at the studio. Only a lucky few are kept safe in a studio archive.

DESIGNING THE PAST AND THE FUTURE

Ruth E. Carter, designer for *Black Panther*, has long worked on productions portraying black history, such as *Malcolm X*, *The Butler*, *Selma*, and the 2016 remake of the TV miniseries *Roots*. She specializes in films, having worked on over forty. That said, she began her career as a costume apprentice for the Santa Fe Opera in New Mexico. Just two years after moving to Los Angeles, she began working with director Spike Lee, with whom she frequently collaborated for over two decades.

In an interview for collider.com's Movie Talk section, Carter discussed her passionate work for *Black Panther*. Drawing on her background and values, she explains that she wanted to "present it in the right way, dispel stereotypes and myths." She rejected prototypes that "looked like costumes," saying, "This is not *The Lion King*, folks! We're going to make this right if I have to lay down and die for it!"

Carter is known for being a stickler for research. When working on *Black Panther*, one entire wall of her workroom was a "vision board" with pictures of various African tribes, their blankets, fabrics, and beads, so her team would work surrounded by a particular look and feel. And yet her intention was not to be literal, but to "move it ahead," into the future.

Importantly, she talks about bringing the depth of African art to the clothes, so that the beadwork

Designer Ruth E. Carter attends the American Black Film Festival Honors Awards in February 2018.

or leatherwork was not merely a stereotype. She was also motivated to "provide images that would speak to all women in a real positive way and help the comic book world to re-imagine … a new way of expressing femininity and power."

A motion capture suit helped place this computerized image of Sandra Bullock into a rocket in the movie *Gravity*.

CHAPTER FOUR

You Can Do This!

C hallenges come in many forms in costume design work. You may have anticipated some of them as you read about important skills to have, or as you read between the lines in the last chapter on the costume design process. For the movie *Gladiator*, 3,500 extras were fit and dressed every day for three months! Of course, you may also know the challenges faced when creating costumes for theater productions for your school or community. For those who are drawn to the field, the challenges get their pulses racing, and they enjoy using their experience and creativity to the max. They love a good challenge because they believe they can win!

While some of the following challenges are not something you can expect to encounter on your amateur or independent productions, they provide real insights into what it takes to work in costuming, as well as some takeaways about skills you can develop to be successful in costuming or any endeavor.

Working with Actors

Working with stars can be both thrilling and challenging. It's not uncommon for them to arrive for their first fitting with their own hair and makeup stylists, or even fashion stylists. Designers need to draw on their diplomatic skills to keep everybody happy.

Some actors only want to be shown racks of clothes by fashion-industry heavyweights like Givenchy, Prada, or Armani. Kym Barrett, who designed *The Matrix*, shares a clever solution: she admits to often removing the labels, so she can sneak in other clothes she is interested in showing an actor. She avoids many arguments this way.

A very different type of challenge occurs when costumes need to be designed before the actor is cast, which is happening more often in this increasingly fast-paced industry. Designer Penny Rose kept nagging about the need to cast a villainous Caribbean pirate for *Pirates of the Caribbean*. When she was finally handed the headshot of an actor selected for the role, she envisioned "a biker pirate." Luckily, when she showed him the leather outfits he'd be wearing in 110-degree-Fahrenheit (43-degree-Celsius) heat while shooting on location in Hawaii, he assented. Rose remembers, "Being British, and a fine actor, he looked at me and said, 'It's not going to be a problem.'"

Pat Welch has designed for several television series, including *L.A. Law* and *Frank's Place* (for which she earned an Emmy nomination), and has mastered the art of working well with actors. First of all, she appreciates that actors are in a sensitive position, because the cinematographer often wants to capture them being vulnerable. She discloses: "I try to make them believe that they are the ones who have the final say. If they really hate a garment, an item, a piece, I'll throw it out. I will not argue. Because I'd rather lose the battle in the dressing room than on the set."

Working with Others

Famous director Oliver Stone was angry at Ellen Mirojnick over the clothing she designed for the character of Gordon Gekko in his movie *Wall Street*. To create a wardrobe for this powerful, provocative stock-market player, she chose silks and cashmeres. Stone protested, "Nobody looks like this on the street." Mirojnick stood her ground, saying, "I don't care. This is what Gordon looks like, and it [the real Wall Street] will look like this eventually." She was right, remarking on the effect that the costumes had on the real Wall Street after the movie became a hit: "It had a terrific influence, changing men's fashion at the time. It gave men permission to be powerful-looking." What's the lesson here? Sometimes you just have to fight for what you know is true.

Contemporary projects can be challenging since today's big movie and television projects have an abundance of what business people call "stakeholders." You've probably noticed that before the title, you'll see quite a list of executive producers, producers, co-producers, and more. Every one of them has an opinion and may be all too eager to advise you, the designer.

With the right set of political skills, including respect, an experienced designer will be able to meet this challenge. Designer Briana Jorgensen has this advice: "The director and the producer want to make their statements. Sometimes they're on the same page and sometimes not … You have to determine very early on who has the power and what you are going to have to do to get everything you know is right for the story and characters. You have to translate what it all means [into] somebody else's vision, without alienating the others."

Working with a Tight Schedule

A limited amount of preparation time and the pace of the shooting schedule are important factors influencing key design decisions. Designers, especially those working in television, have to learn tricks of the trade that will help them keep "up to speed." For your own design work, you may want to use this pair of tricks or shortcuts: provide a jacket or coat to hide poorly fitting garments, and create or choose garments with knit fabrics because they readily adjust to the body.

However, those tricks were no help to designer Carlo Poggioli, who needed to make masses of costumes for the film *Divergent.* After making the prototypes in Rome, where the designer lives, he brought them to workshops in Hungary and Romania. In just one month, thousands of costumes were created for two of the film's social divisions, or factions: the Dauntless (brave) and the Abnegation (selfless).

Thousands of costumes were made for actors in the movie *Divergent*, down to the belts and bracelets.

Huge Background

The background talent (who do not have speaking parts) needs to be dressed with the same care as the actors with speaking parts. They are all actors, playing a part, and need to be dressed according to character. They are part of the environments that create the world being filmed.

In the scene of the Choosing Ceremony in *Divergent*, seven hundred extras from all the different factions were required. Each of their handmade costumes was finished in Chicago—where the film was being shot—after being fitted to each extra or actor. This story might motivate you to believe you can handle a cast of twenty or even fifty. Keep records, keep organized, keep calm, keep your sense of humor, and find people to help you!

Even if the costumes are not tailor-made to each individual extra, every background actor must be styled by a set costumer. You may begin to pay closer attention to scenes with large crowds, such as the Snow Ball in *Stranger Things* or school scenes in *Pretty Little Liars*. Each of those background actors needed to have their costume styled by a set costumer before they were filmed. An experienced set costumer may be expected to style a dozen extras each hour. It's not called "speed styling" for nothing! Typically, everyone needs to look different from each other yet consistent within character subgroups. Successful designers meet the challenge by being creative, laser-focused, and flexible.

You can't assume that the extras will remain in the background. Pat Welch, who has vast experience styling TV shows, advises: "The camera can pick them out, and you can get horrible surprises. Or the director will fall in love with someone in the background, a wonderful character, and bring him right up to the camera."

One tactic costumers use to make working with extras more efficient is to collaborate with the casting agency that hired them. For example, designers may request that the thirty extras who will play Chicago police officers will all be within a certain height and weight range.

Managing a huge wardrobe requires following standard organizing principles, or everyone will be stressed:

- Hang all items facing the same direction.

- Hang all pants full-length.

- Note the sizes of similar costume pieces by placing a tag in the same location for each item (ideally, the upper, outermost corner of the garment).

- Hang similar costume pieces in order of size, from small to large.

- Arrange costumes in order of the performer's importance, from stars and principals to secondary lead characters and featured day players.

Out of Stock The year 2016 marked the beginning of what critics called "peak TV." That was the year in which a record-breaking 455 new series were shown across broadcast, cable, and streaming services like Netflix, Hulu, and Amazon Prime. That's more than double what it had been a decade earlier. One genre that has been particularly popular is period dramas. Period dramas are often called "costume dramas" because the costumes play such an important role in their appeal. Think *Downton Abbey*, *The Crown*, or *Poldark*.

The popularity of period dramas is great for scriptwriters, actors, directors, and others who are happy to have jobs doing work they love. But it presents a major challenge for designers, since they're the ones charged with acquiring the costumes. Notes Tim Angel, head of Angel Costumes: "It's been to a level we haven't seen before: You could start with one film set in the 1800s, and I guarantee by the end of four weeks' time, there'll be another three productions all in the same period. You can't just go off to the street and find [those vintage clothes]."

So what do you do if a costume supplier you have depended upon in the past is "out of stock," or that great vintage clothing store has just sold its last 1950s ball gown dress, the one with the white rhinestones in front? The lesson here for amateur and independent productions: think ahead. If you have a limited budget, don't commit to costumes you can't afford to make, borrow, or rent. Time and budget restrictions are real, and sticking to your commitments is a great muscle to work.

Designing for Stunt Work

The costume designer consults with the stunt coordinator for guidance on the stunts and destructive action, since the color, shape, material, and style of clothing will be affected. Actor Kathleen Turner needed a suit to wear while crashing through the Colombian jungles with Michael Douglas in the 1984 film *Romancing the Stone*. Rather than pick a durable fabric, designer Marilyn Vance designed a suit made of tussah silk, since she knew it would quickly begin to get rips and tears and basically "self-distress." Brilliant! She used "lateral thinking" to find a unique solution. Instead of making multiples that would need to be distressed to appear like the suit was getting ragged, she chose just the opposite.

Experienced designers know that stunt work involving things like fire and gunshot effects typically requires natural fibers rather than synthetics like rayon, which would melt. To create a gunshot effect, a small explosive device called a "squib" is attached under a specific spot on the fabric of a shirt, for example. The spot will have been sandpapered to be thin, so that when the squib explodes, the shirt is quickly torn and blackened.

Designers also know that stuntmen for action heroes will require outfits that appear identical to what the stars are wearing, but are actually made larger to accommodate special padding and flying rigs. Flexible shoes are also part of the must-haves for stunt choreography. What shoes do your actors need to wear to take flight when the director calls, "Action!"?

Designing for a Script Based on a Book

American novelist Veronica Roth was writing *Allegiant*, the third book in her science-fiction trilogy, when production started on the movie version of *Divergent*, the first book. Roth and director Neil Burger came to a common agreement about the time period (about 150 years in the future), which was a critical decision for costume design. They informed designer Carlo Poggioli about the time period and the colors of each social division in the book's imagined world. He would need to come up with the shapes of the clothes and other specifics.

The Hunger Games and its sequels also needed translation as they moved from book to screen. In the books, every tribute from every district wears the same thing to the games, signaling that they are all equal. Explains designer Makovsky: "That's fine in a book, but not in a film [because] you're not going to know who anybody is if everybody's in a black jacket." The director decided that each district would have its own color jacket.

Superheroes

In fantasy and action genres, the costume and the character are closely associated. Movies and TV shows featuring superheroes undergo the greatest scrutiny of costumes by the fans of the novel, comics, or games on which they are based. Those fans have strong expectations about how the superheroes look; in many ways, the costume is the character.

While fans want the film version of their character to look just like they expect, they also want the superheroes to look cool by today's standards. The challenge for the costume designer of superheroes is to be true to the original and yet update the look. Three-time Oscar winner Colleen Atwood, known for her work designing costumes for *The Flash*, *Arrow*, and *Supergirl*, had this to say about the challenges she faces: "With the superheroes I've been doing, the idea is to give them street cred while paying homage to their roots."

Batman and *Superman* comic strips were created over seventy years ago. Giving them a contemporary, buzzworthy look is no easy task. "It's an amazing, broad, and complex experience," says Oscar nominee Michael Wilkinson, the costume designer behind *Man of Steel* and *Batman v Superman: Dawn of Justice*. In addition to the director and costume design team, illustrators, production designers, visual effects artists, stunt teams, fabric specialists, and specialty costume manufacturers are all involved in building a suit. "It is a massive collaboration," says Alexandra Byrne, the Oscar-winning costume designer for *Thor*, *Guardians of the Galaxy*, and the *Avengers* series of films.

First, the designer must understand the director's vision for the superhero movie or TV show. Will it be a modern-day rendition like *Agents of S.H.I.E.L.D.* or will it be stylized in some way, like the retro feel of *Guardians of the Galaxy*? The research process may require the costume designer to study a broad range of subjects. Designing for *Black Panther*, for example, entailed studying African fabrics and patterns as well as the anticipated future of high-tech.

Prototypes are often created early in the process. Atwood explains her process this way:

> *Usually, the first prototype tells me enough that by the time I get to the second one, I'm in decent shape ... and then [we add] all the details. On a superhero, you show all the details ahead of time to the studio and the comic companies and make sure that they're cool with all the stuff that you've changed up a bit from your concept drawing to make the costume work.*

Footwear design is particularly important for the superhero, since you want your hero to look fantastic yet avoid slipping while chasing a villain. For Grant Gustin, who plays The Flash, Atwood designed several pairs of footwear. She hired a boot maker to create what she calls "the statue pair," designed to look terrific while The Flash is just standing around. For racing, which The Flash does a lot, she built a shoe *over* the shoes that he had been using while training. Notice how she reframed the problem from "replacing his own shoes with new shoes" to "letting his training shoes *look like* new shoes."

When designers are working from comic book material, such as the Marvel universe, they engage in a new type of research. They dig into the backstories of the characters, so they can incorporate even small things that make each character unique. Fans of *Agents of S.H.I.E.L.D.* are known for being very protective of their favorite characters, giving designer Ann Foley feedback on Twitter; collaboration now extends to viewers, who go online to express their likes and dislikes about costumes.

Foley is up to the challenge of dealing with an active fan base for superheroes. "This is their show," she says. "These are their characters, so I really try to give the fans something to be excited about."

Costume designer Michael Wilkinson, who designed the Batsuit that actor Ben Affleck wore as Batman, says he likes being part of the online discussion. "It's no longer a designer just in his workroom pushing a costume out into the world and that's it," he says. "There's a real sense of a conversation and engaging in a dialogue about this stuff."

The twenty-first-century revised costumes for Batman, Wonder Woman, and Aquaman were all unleashed into the world not through studio press releases but via director Zack Snyder's tweets.

Working with CGI

The growth of computer-generated imagery (CGI) and of motion-capture (mocap) can be seen as a challenging trend except for those who enjoy learning and adapting to new technologies. When working with CGI, designers have to be aware of constraints imposed by new technology and of changes that happen during postproduction. CGI has gone through some amazing developments since its original use in the movie *Who Framed Roger Rabbit* in 1988. More recent films like *Avatar* and *Spider-Man: Homecoming* demonstrate just how far CGI has traveled since computer-generated imagery first hit the big screen.

In the 2017 adaptation of *Beauty and the Beast*, Oscar-winning designer Jacqueline Durran needed to create a costume for the Beast. Originally, the design concept was to build a prosthetic that British actor Dan Stevens would wear. It was only after the Beast's costumes had been designed and construction had begun that the decision was made to use CGI instead. The special effects department, armed not only with actual garments but also patterns and fabrics, used them to digitally build the Beast. As the character develops in the story, his clothing progresses from a ragged cloak to a fine coat and sleeved waistcoat—accomplished with the "magic" of CGI.

Actually working with CGI might be something you will eventually do if you pursue your interest in costume design. For now, you can prepare yourself for this exciting challenge by learning about the latest developments in CGI technology and by feeding your passion for new ideas.

Product Placement

In *Stranger Things*, when Eleven is shown grabbing boxes of Eggo waffles from the freezer, it is an instance of "product placement."

Product placement also happens with clothing and fashion accessories on television and in the movies. Unless you recognize the clothing line (like Abercrombie) or see the brand name or logo (like Nike's swoosh), you won't realize how much of it is going on. Professionals called "fashion publicists" work to get their client's gear placed on film and television. Clothing manufacturers may pay the production company if the principal actors wear their brands, or they may provide items as gifts or loans. Any of these arrangements will help the bottom line (i.e., the budget), so designers can be under real pressure from the producers to utilize product placement.

Oscar-nominee Jeffrey Kurland, costume designer for *Ocean's Eleven*, used his experience to say how he felt about product placement: "Right from the start I made it clear that I was not interested in making this a retail extravaganza, or speaking to a plethora of suit manufacturers who might want to dress George Clooney or Brad Pitt." Director Steven Soderbergh agreed with Kurland that the film "required a certain theatricality," and endorsed Kurland's choice of superb outfits that help elevate the story to comedy. Kurland explains: "Our job was to lift the drama above reality: although it had to look real, [Soderbergh's] plan was to heighten the narrative through his direction."

How can product placement help you in your own costuming? While looking for clothes for an upcoming

production, ask local retailers if they will give you
or loan you clothes in exchange for screen credit and
publicity. Some aspiring designers might be tempted
to buy brand-new clothes, use them, and then return
them, hoping to get a refund. But that's a strategy that
lacks integrity, besides being dishonest. Any designer
who tries it is likely to earn a reputation as someone
not to be trusted.

TV Productions

Costume designers working in film often complain
about never having enough time to get the job done.
However, designers in television argue that their job
is harder because they are under much more pressure
than their colleagues in film. They point out that in
television, budgets are limited—meaning, insufficient
to create what the designer believes is required to
tell the story. You're now familiar with one tactic for
staying within a limited budget: product placement.

Another source of the pressure is very tight
schedules. More pages of TV script are shot each day
compared to the shooting schedule for movies. TV
productions are often called "shop jobs" because the
designers often send staff out to the stores to buy
what's needed instead of creating it in-house.

As discussed in chapter 3, if a costume is going to
look like something a character really owns and wears,
then it needs to be aged or distressed. In television,
there is not enough time or money to do either of
those—not even launder the clothes. This results in
shows with a "catalog look" of chronic newness and
overly trendy styles. As an amateur designer, you

can take a good look at the wardrobe you have put together and see how you might treat or stylize the pieces so they don't look brand new.

Another challenge designers face with TV productions is that the directors are more likely to shoot close-up, such as characters sitting at a dinner table. The camera in close-up will tend to emphasize whatever is framing the face. For example, shoulder pads—whether in a man's suit or a woman's dress—can make necks disappear. When designing wardrobes for your own cast, be aware of which characters will be shot in a close-up, and pay special attention to what surrounds their face, such as earrings, necklaces, glasses, hats, collars, and scarves.

"A Gas and a Half"

Given all the challenges of costuming for movies and television, why do it? Holly Cole and Kristin Burke, writing in *Costuming for Film: The Art and the Craft*, answer this way: "It's a gas and a half. As hairy as the production process sounds, it is not impossible. It's like moving to a big city: You just start to move faster, naturally … Most of all, you have to have passion."

KIDS AND HATS

Costume designer Jaci Rohr, experienced in both television and movies, tells this story of a real challenge that happened on her very first movie.

Her first job was as a set costumer, which is the person responsible for getting everyone dressed exactly right. For that day's shoot, that meant about five principals and twenty-five extras. And she had exactly no one to help her.

As luck would have it, they were shooting on a very rainy day—and of course, the costume trailer was a long three blocks away from the set.

A child actor had been wearing a red knit stocking cap with a pom-pom on top and a name on the front. Walking with the boy and his mom back to the set, Rohr realized he was missing his hat! The hat had already been on camera and, of course, there were no doubles.

In a great panic, she ran back to the designer, crying because she expected to be fired. Instead, the designer calmly looked in the sock drawer. Finding a red sock, the costumer quickly cut it, then made and sewed on a pom-pom. Rohr rushed back to the set through the downpour, hoping that no one would notice the name was missing.

Since then, Rohr has worked her way up the ladder in costumes. Her résumé shows her past positions. Before becoming a costume designer, she worked as a costumer, on-set costumer, extras set costumer, wardrobe assistant, wardrobe coordinator, costume supervisor, and assistant costume designer.

This dress became a trendsetter after being worn by Audrey Hepburn in *Sabrina*.

CHAPTER FIVE

Dream Big

The challenges we've been talking about may have you more excited about costume design. Or maybe they are making you want to know what other things you can do after you've spent time in the field.

Degrees and Internships

Let's start first with those of you who are feeling "Yeah, this is for me!" We've been talking about activities you can pursue while in middle school and high school. There are colleges and universities—both in the United States and abroad—that offer a bachelor's degree with a major in costume design. Associate's degrees and master's degrees are also available.

If you major in costume design, you'll learn how to design, select, and build costumes for characters in plays and other types of performances. In addition to sketching and building costumes of your own design, you'll study theory and criticism, period styles, and how to analyze scripts to determine costuming choices.

Why wait? Start looking now for a costume internship in a summer stock theater festival, community or regional theater, or other venue. Your local TV stations and ad agencies are also worth checking out. This is an opportunity to learn from experienced people while working on one or more productions. Also, start putting together a portfolio of any costumes you design yourself.

What to Learn Now

Internships will give you hands-on experience in the art of costume design. But another great source of information are books and websites in which designers discuss their work and share their knowledge and insights. Here are four topics you can begin exploring to get you started in costume design:

- **Knowledge of historical periods.** What did people wear in New York in the 1920s, Edwardian England, fourteenth-century Persia, or sixteenth-century China? "People" includes all classes of people and not just the nobility or upper class. The internet will connect you to vast collections of images and patterns; check out the For More Information section in the back of this book to begin your exploration.

- **Knowledge of art.** A director may say that she wants "the whole palette to be Monet" and expect you to know she means colors like those found in paintings by the French impressionist Claude Monet. The practice of referring to visual art, such as paintings, makes sense when you remember that "movies" are "moving pictures." The director, cinematographer, production designer, set designer, and set dresser are all thinking about how each frame looks. You can develop your knowledge of art by taking art classes, visiting art galleries, and reading illustrated art books. Then try to link the costume designs in specific movies or TV shows with the work of artists with whom you're familiar.

• **Knowledge of color.** Designers use color to provoke emotion, clarify personality, control focus, and emphasize alliances and conflicts among characters and the worlds in which they move. Of all the compositional elements of design, color has perhaps the greatest potential to express emotions. You can develop an eye for color by watching some of your favorite films or TV series with the sound turned off. What color palette did the designers use? What emotions do the colors make you feel? Imagine putting an important character in a contrasting color. How would that change viewers' perceptions about their personality?

Below is an abbreviated chart linking different color palettes with common associations. You may have fun identifying movies or shows that utilize each:

Palette	Associations
bold, intense colors	lively environment, forceful personalities
muted, neutralized colors	subdued atmosphere, passive personalities
dark palette	dramatic, tragic, powerful
light palette	comic or romantic
warm colors	comfortable, relaxed, safe
cool colors	emotional chilliness
warm dark colors	weighty, earthy
pale tints	airy, whimsical, fantasy

- **Knowledge of fabrics.** Until the 1920s, fabrics were only made of natural fibers like wool and cotton. It wasn't until the 1960s that stretch fabrics—polyesters, synthetic knits, and metallic fabrics—became available. Suppose the show you're working on is set in the 1920s and you need to dress actors playing flappers (young, carefree women of the time). By choosing silk rather than rayon for their costumes, you'll be staying true to the period.

Additionally, you'll want to learn about what the texture of a fabric communicates. Texture refers to the way a fabric feels when you touch it. Even if you've already seen it, watch *The Lord of the Rings* for a fantastic demonstration of the ability of fabric to communicate. Galadriel, played by Cate Blanchett, fairly floats in her incredibly light fabrics, while the hobbits are wearing natural fabrics with really strong weaves to convey an organic earthiness. Browsing high-end, or upscale, clothing stores will heighten your awareness of the differences between designer-label and off-the-rack clothing. The biggest difference is the quality of the fabric.

Volunteering to work in a costume workroom for your school or community theater may introduce you to fabrics you've never seen. By working with experienced costumers, you'll discover that, for them, the word "sewing" is not really appropriate to what they do. Instead, it is called "constructing" or "building" because so much more can go into the final costume.

Pathways into Costuming

Let's look at some of the diverse pathways that have brought people into costume design. Howard Sussman, costume supervisor for *Dancing with the Stars*, earned his degree in merchandising, followed by executive training at Macy's department store. He was able to get into the costumer's union after working at a costume rental facility. On the TV series *Moonlighting*, Sussman worked as a shopper: "You get in on a show and you work your way up from assisting to supervising. I could've become a designer if I had those aspirations." Notice two things about Sussman's story: like nearly everyone in the field, he had to work his way up, and not everyone wants to be a designer.

Costume designer
Sharen Davis

Sharen Davis studied acting, then worked in the art department of a movie studio, followed by seven years as a costume supervisor before designing five films. Janty Yates went to dress design school to learn design, dressmaking, and pattern cutting. She then worked in a wholesale fashion house and designed patterns for Vogue and Butterick. She also assisted on commercials and designed some herself.

Michael Kaplan received a scholarship to study drawing and sculpture at the Philadelphia College of Art. After graduation, he designed book jackets and worked in commercial graphic design. Fascinated by fashion from the age of four, Kaplan moved to Los Angeles and worked as an illustrator for legendary television designers Bob Mackie and Ret Turner. He also designed a stage show for singer-actress Bette Midler.

Judianna Makovsky studied art (painting, textile arts, drawing) and theater. She designed costumes for operas and theaters before realizing she really wanted to design for film.

Ellen Mirojnick worked as the head designer of Happy Legs, a ready-to-wear clothing company. "One of the owners was an important mentor. He taught me how to work with people, how to be myself and how not to compromise about my gut feelings, while still paying attention to others, to business, and to what sells." Mirojnick designed a couple of commercials, which helped her land a costuming job in *Fatal Attraction*, her first movie.

While costume design is a very specific process with well-defined roles, the work habits and skills that you develop will prepare you for positions in a variety of fields outside of costuming.

Exploring Show Biz

Entertainment is a very broad field with many related occupations. In addition to designing for film and television, you might consider working as a costumer for theater productions, commercials, or music videos. How about designing for dance, opera, ice shows, or even the circus? To dress the 1,300 artists appearing in Cirque du Soleil shows, which offer a modern type of circus with outrageous costumes and no animals, designers maintain their own costume workshop employing over three hundred specialists in shoemaking, textile design, lace-making, costume-making, and millinery (hats). Costume-makers include patternmakers, textile designers, dyers, stitchers, tailors, and more.

If your interest is less about costumes than the overall look of the movie or show, you may want to become a set designer, set decorator, or production designer. One interesting responsibility under the production designer is location scouting, where your job is to find the city, neighborhoods, or other locations that match the director's vision for a particular scene.

Another possible route for you to consider is cinematography. The story of cinematographer Shane Hurlbut tells a lot about how a successful journey may be a winding road. Hurlbut began his interest in entertainment while reading the morning announcements for his high school; fellow students told him he had a great voice for radio. At a two-year college, he worked hard studying first radio and then television. His dedication paid off with a full scholarship to major in film at Emerson College in Boston, Massachusetts.

Despite graduating magna cum laude—awarded to students at the top of their class—Hurlbut needed to start at the bottom of the film industry and work his way up. He drove a truck for a costume rental house, then gripped for a producer. (A grip is a member of the camera crew working with the equipment that supports cameras and helps shape the light.) Hurlbut also worked on music videos and editorial photography for such magazines as *Vanity Fair.* These diverse but related experiences prepared him to become the director of photography (DP) on *The Rat Pack* for HBO.

What can you learn from this story? Explore, keep learning, say yes, network, and pay attention to what excites you. To get more ideas about possibilities, check out the book *Hire Me, Hollywood!: Your Behind-the-Scenes Guide to the Most Exciting—and Unexpected—Jobs in Show Business.*

If the latest technology is your passion, then you might want to investigate special effects manufacturing. There may be opportunities for you to join a group of "costume prop specialists" who work with or develop new manufacturing techniques, materials, and technologies, including computer-aided design (CAD) to make costumes as realistic, lightweight, comfortable, and strong as possible. For more information on careers in special effects and universities that offer training, check out learn.org.

Additionally, there is the growing application of CGI for costume design. See the For More Information section for a link to an example from *Beauty and the Beast*.

Helpful high school courses include:

- Theater Arts, Performing Arts

- Studio Art, Art History, Design

- Computer-Assisted Design (CAD), Computer Multimedia Arts

- Photography, Commercial Photography

- Film and Video Production

- Drawing, Visual Arts, Graphic Design, Digital Art Imaging

Exploring Fashion

Do you enjoy shopping and have an eye for what's hot and what's not? Do you look forward to flipping through the pages of your favorite fashion magazines? Then the role of purchasing agent could be a potential career path. Purchasing agents buy products for organizations to use or resell. Retailers will value your skills if you have a knack for knowing what people want now, or want next. Costume designer Molly Rogers, who won an Emmy for her work on the TV series *Sex and the City*, worked for clothing stores in London and New York before she started styling artists for music videos. That led to her freelance job as a costume designer for commercials, television, and movies.

To develop your interest in fashion and/or design, you may want to start your own blog as a personal stylist or a fashion blogger. Becoming a personal shopper is also an interesting way of being involved with fashion and using your eye for style.

If creativity is what really excites you, and you would rather not have to deal with directors or scripts, you may want to Google these helpful organizations: Council of Fashion Designers of America, The Business of Fashion, the National Association of Schools of Art and Design, and O*NET. For example, go to ONetOnLine.org and search for "designer" to find not only fashion designer but another nineteen related occupations. Click on Fashion Designers and you'll get a comprehensive introduction to the tasks, technology skills, knowledge, abilities, and work activities, as well as the work styles and work values typical for this role. You can also browse the O*NET site for other occupations based on your interests, abilities, or other factors.

Great Qualities

When you work on costuming at school, with friends, or with groups from your community, you'll develop some great skills. These prepare you for a range of opportunities beyond costume design. Here are some of these prized qualities:

- **Upbeat.** Fun to work with. Known for having a positive attitude.

- **Good listener.** Can read "body language." Body language can provide you with clues as to how others are feeling. For example, crossed arms often signal that the person is feeling defensive.

- **Flexible.** You may have designed, constructed, and fitted a garment you're crazy about, only to learn the role has been cut at the last minute or the shot will simply be a close-up. Your ability to be flexible is mightily enhanced if you have learned to not only have a plan A but a plan B and plan C.

- **Good communicator.** Designers need to make presentations to the director to get his or her approval at several points during preproduction. Use the opportunities in both classes and theater to practice speaking up comfortably and convincingly.

- **Get along well with others.** In costume design, you need to win the confidence of people above you, the cooperation of people alongside you, and the respect of people who report to you. In addition, you have to have a thick skin, which means being able to take criticism and not become defensive.

- **Respectful, empathetic.** Your school or community theater experience as an actor can help you gain the confidence of the actors you will be dressing. Oscar-nominee Sharen Davis credits her acting experience for enabling her to be considered "a treasured creative partner" as she worked on *Dreamgirls*, *The Help*, and *Ray*.

- **Willing to start from the bottom and help out as needed.** Before Michael Kaplan became such a successful designer in Hollywood, he was running errands and doing odd jobs for the costume department of the 1970s *Sonny & Cher Show*. "I worked for all of them doing things like coloring shoes to match dresses, or shopping for buttons ... An amazing education!" For school or community film or TV productions, be willing to wash T-shirts or iron dresses, as well as the more fun things like shopping in vintage clothing stores.

- **Courageous.** Judianna Makovsky, winner of a Career Achievement Award from the Costume Designers Guild, talks about how she overcame her fears and achieved what she set out to do: "My most challenging films were *The Hunger Games* and *Harry Potter* ... Trying to get the director's vision and at the same time keep true to the essence of the book is terrifying for a designer ... What if I had designed Dumbledore wrong? People would hate me! I have to admit, I'm very proud that I designed the first *Harry Potter* movie and established those now-legendary characters."

New Possibilities

Having trained your eye, you may want to think more broadly about where you can use your ability to visualize. The whole field of art direction values an eye for detail and the ability to visualize with imagination. A rich resource is the book *Careers in Art*. It provides an overview of a range of art-related careers in television and theater as well as interior design for homes, offices, and retail space, plus exhibit and display design.

Graphic designers create visual concepts—using computer software or by hand—to communicate ideas that inspire, inform, and captivate consumers. They develop the overall layout and production design for various applications such as advertisements, brochures, magazines, and websites.

In their book *Firestarters*, Kelly Beatty and Dale Salvaggio Bradshaw provide "one hundred job profiles to inspire young women." They profile Louanne DiBella, who is a jewelry and product designer and product development specialist. The TV series *Shark Tank* also features many entrepreneurs pitching their new products, including fashion and accessories. You can learn a lot about business and have fun predicting whom the "sharks" will find worthy of their investment dollars.

Worthy Advice

We've covered a lot about the art and craft of costuming for film and television. Because it's an exciting field filled with creative, dynamic people, the competition to get in and be successful may seem scary. So let's close with some advice from Molly Rogers, designer for *Sex and the City*.

> *Dream big! Whatever you think is possible is truly possible ... As small or large a task may be, take pride and learn from everything and everyone you encounter ... Having an open, nonjudgmental mind can give you opportunities that will ultimately benefit you in all aspects of your life.*

It's encouraging to remember that the television and movie industry is filled with creative, energetic people who are passionate about the work they are doing. They can look at the finished product, know that it will be seen by countless people, and say, "I had a hand in that!" Whether you choose to pursue costume design or some other role, you've given yourself a solid introduction to this fascinating business.

COSPLAY

Cosplay, or "costume play," is a unique way to enjoy costuming. In cosplay, people create and wear costumes from a TV show, movie, or a character from a book, video game, web comic, anime (Japanese animated show), manga (Japanese comic book), or other form of entertainment. Cosplay began in the mid-1980s as fans wore costumes to science-fiction conventions. If you venture into a convention near you, expect to see characters you may not recognize, unless you are also into anime and manga.

One of the fun things about cosplay is the opportunity to behave like someone other than yourself. Princess Jasmine from Disney's *Aladdin* has a strength that you might like to try on for size. Dressing like Lara Croft from the video game *Tomb Raider* lets girls behave in a very bold, determined way. Exploring other ways of acting develops "emotional literacy"—the ability to understand and express feelings—as well as a greater appreciation for the impact costumes have on actors. Cosplay requires a mix of smart thrift store shopping, sewing, prop making, makeup application, and learning how to pose and behave in character. Learning how to do all of that is more fun if you can join or start a club at your school. In the summer of 2017, the city of Brookline in Massachusetts offered weekly cosplay workshops for teens. Being able to use the library resources allowed participants to study cinematic art books and recommended YouTube channels and websites. In fact, one participant was able to use their 3D printer to create a Doctor Doom mask.

GLOSSARY

arc The emotional journey of the story and that of the key characters. Costumes change to signal the characters' internal changes.

color palette The set of colors that will be used for filming, such as darks, pastels, or neons.

computer-generated imagery (CGI) Any digital effect, including computer animation of monsters, fierce storms, and including both human-like characters and costumes.

costume Any piece of clothing, whether it is borrowed, rented, or purchased, or built just for the production.

costume breakdown A listing of the costume changes for every single character in every scene.

costumer The person responsible for dressing the actors, ironing, laundry, continuity, and creating the costume department on location. In theater, this person is called a "dresser."

costume stock The general store of costumes at the studio or costume rental house.

costume supervisor The managing director of the costume department and the close partner of the designer.

cutter A person who enhances every costume by suggesting the best fabric, lining, and trims. Also called a fitter.

distress To make clothing look as old and worn as the script demands. It is also called aging or breaking down.

extra An actor who has no lines, such as a pedestrian, diner, or army solider, that is needed to complete the scene and provide context. Also called atmosphere or background.

flying rig A system of ropes, pulleys, and related devices to enable actors to appear to be flying.

grip A member of the crew responsible for building and maintaining all of the equipment that supports cameras, such as placing a camera dolly on a track for a smooth moving shot.

mood board A collage of inspiration that costume designers, directors, and production designers use to communicate their vision.

multiple In costuming, the term essentially means "copy."

period Any time in the past other than the present, even if it is relatively recent like the 1980s or 1990s.

production company The largest are Universal Studios, Walt Disney Studios, and Warner Brothers Studios. Also called a production house.

product placement Deliberately including a product (such as a pair of Nikes) to promote a brand.

pull To select garments from stock, whether at a studio's wardrobe collection or at a costume rental house.

wardrobe A synonym for "costume," as in "wardrobe department."

FOR MORE INFORMATION

Books

Cole, Holly, and Kristin Burke. *Costuming for Film: The Art and The Craft.* Los Angeles: Silman-James Press, 2005.

Egan, Kate. *The Hunger Games: The Official Illustrated Movie Companion.* New York: Scholastic Press, 2012.

Jorgensen, Jay, and Donald L. Scoggins. *Creating the Illusion: A Fashionable History of Hollywood Costume Designers.* Philadelphia, PA: Running Press Book Publishers, 2015.

LaMotte, Richard. *Costume Design 101: The Business and Art of Creating Costumes for Film and Television.* 2nd ed. Studio City, CA: Michael Wiese Productions, 2010.

Landis, Deborah Nadoolman, ed. *Costume Design.* Waltham, MA: Focal Press, 2012.

———. *Hollywood Costume.* New York: Abrams, 2013.

Sibley, Brian. *The Hobbit: An Unexpected Journey Official Movie Guide*. Boston, MA: Houghton Mifflin Harcourt, 2012.

Websites

Ann Foley Design

http://www.annfoleydesign.com

This is the official website of Ann Foley (designer for Marvel's *Agents of S.H.I.E.L.D.*). Go to the Press tab to read how she creates superhero costumes and her list of other costume designers to follow on social media.

Cameron Dale

http://www.camerondale.com

Cameron Dale has designed for the hit series *Pretty Little Liars*. Check out her Instagram at cameroncostumes or her tweets @camifdale.

Clothes on Film

https://clothesonfilm.com/where-am-i

This website features over four hundred essays and interviews with the best designers.

Costume Designers Guild

https://www.costumedesignersguild.com

This is the Costume Designers Guild website. Click on Articles for both articles and videos, or on the Resources tab for industry links.

Motion Picture Costumers IATSE Local 705

https://www.motionpicturecostumers.org

This website features a look at movie costume designers.

Videos

Alice in Wonderland: Fashion and Style
https://www.youtube.com/watch?v=tAlTsIAH9lE
In this video, designer Colleen Atwood takes you through her process.

Animated Skinsuit *Green Lantern* Featurette
https://www.youtube.com/watch?v=7Kce36cJZDY
This video includes footage of the superhero's suit testing and development for the movie *Green Lantern.*

Costume CO: The Analysis of Cinematic Costume
https://www.youtube.com/channel/UCtkJUNxVlcy-uFSsn32hKKg/videos
Costume CO is a YouTube channel that presents detailed analyses of costumes from selected popular television shows and movies.

Costume Design Basics: A Process Tutorial
https://www.youtube.com/watch?v=JXhxVVTe9xA
Find out in this video how to make costumes.

The Costume Designers
https://www.youtube.com/watch?v=-dCtt_3TA84
This hour-long interview explores the world of five of the biggest names in costume design.

The Costumes of *Stranger Things*
https://www.youtube.com/watch?v=iwWNrFFYh8I
This video includes mood boards for six characters.

Dan Stevens Without CGI in *Beauty and the Beast*
https://www.youtube.com/watch?v=0Wcd_EkJyNw
Watch "Beast" Dan Stevens in his motion-capture suit
on the set of *Beauty and the Beast*.

Online Articles

Barnes, Bronwyn. "*Big Bang Theory* Fashion Explained!"
    Entertainment. http://ew.com/article/2012/11/29/
    big-bang-theory-fashion-explained.

Brannigan, Maura. "How *Harry Potter* Costume
    Designer Jany Temime Created a World of Magic
    Through Clothing." *Fashionista*. June 13, 2017.
    https://fashionista.com/2017/06/jany-temime-harry-
    potter-costume-designer-interview.

Gray, Ali. "A Brief History of Motion-Capture
    in the Movies." IGN. http://www.ign.com/
    articles/2014/07/11/a-brief-history-of-motion-
    capture-in-the-movies.

Gurst, Lexi. "*Harry Potter*: Behind the Seams." *Daily
    Geekette*. August 1, 2015. https://dailygeekette.
    wordpress.com/2015/08/01/harry-potter-behind-
    the-seams.

Landis, Deborah Nadoolman. "The Role of Costume
    Designers." Mastering Film. Accessed March 13,
    2018. http://masteringfilm.com/the-role-of-
    costumes-and-costume-designers.

Moore, Booth. "From Haute Couture to Hot
Rods: *The Last Jedi* Costume Designer on His
Inspiration." *Hollywood Reporter.* December 18, 2017.
https://www.hollywoodreporter.com/news/last-jedi-
costume-designer-his-inspiration-1068776.

Pardes, Arielle. "9 Things I Wish I Knew Before I
Became a Costume Designer." *Cosmopolitan.* January
24, 2017. http://www.cosmopolitan.com/career/
a8634552/costume-designer-career-things-i-wish-
i-knew.

Ryzik, Melana. "The Afrofuturistic Designs of *Black
Panther.*" *New York Times.* February 23, 2018.
https//www.nytimes.com/2018/02/23/movies/black-
panther-afrofuturism-costumes-ruth-carter.html.

Sommers, Kate. "WATCH: Dan Stevens Reveals How
He Was Transformed into a Beast." BBC America.
February 2017. http://www.bbcamerica.com/
anglophenia/2017/02/watch-dan-stevens-reveals-
how-he-was-transformed-into-a-beast.

Soo Hoo, Fawnia, "How Superhero Costumes Are
Made." *Fashionista.* March 31, 2015. https://
fashionista.com /2015/03/superhero-costume-design.

INDEX

Page numbers in **boldface** are illustrations

grip, 19, 78

hair and makeup, 14, 24–25, 54

high school, options while in, 8, 82, 85

Hunger Games, The, 8–9, 61, 82

Kaplan, Michael, 9, 13, 20, 41, 76, 82

lighting, 19–20, 35, 42–43

Makovsky, Judianna, 8–9, 14, 24, 62, 76, 82

mood board, 13, **28**, 32, 35

multiple, 36, 38, 41, 60

period, 9, 13–14, 24, 31, 32–34, 60–61, 71–72, 74

period dramas, 5, 59

photo double, 36, 38

Pirates of the Caribbean, 20, **21**, 31, 54

postproduction, 65

preproduction, 29–30, 42, 81

producer, 15, 17–18, 32, 44, 55–56, 66, 78

production company, 49, 66

production designer, 9, 17–19, 25, 32, 35, 63, 73, 77

product placement, 18, 66–67

pull, 30, 38, 40, **49**

research, 24, 31–33, 50, 63–64

Rose, Penny, 20–21, 54

sewing, 5, 27, 33, 39, 75, 85

Star Wars, 6, 9, **15**

Stranger Things, 8, 10, 24–25, 32, 41, 58, 66

stunt double, 7, 36–38, 60–61, 63

superhero, 5, 62–64

wardrobe, 7, 10, 17, 19, 27, **28**, 30, 38, 47, 55, 58, 68–69

working with actors, 10–11, 20–22, 44, 48, 54–55

working with writers, 23–24

ABOUT THE AUTHOR

Nancy Capaccio is a writer, researcher, actor, and former teacher. She has had leading roles in several stage plays as well as in the feature-length independent movie *Manual*, directed by Garth Donovan. She is very experienced in performing and teaching Playback Theatre, a form of improvisation dedicated to helping people share their stories.